A PHILOSOPHY OF DELIGHT

We have to use our wits
in contending with the
conditions of our exist-
ence, but we may be
intuitively aware that this
is only a fragmentary
interpretation of a reality
about which our ordinary
attitudes remain ignorant.
It may then become pos-
sible amidst the other
activities of everyday life,
to cultivate a practical
awareness of this much
deeper reality.

A PHILOSOPHY OF DELIGHT

by
J.H. Reyner
B.Sc.,C.Eng.,F.I.E.E.

WATKINS · LONDON
Publishers & Booksellers

First impression 1976

Produced and distributed by
Watkins Publishing
45 Lower Belgrave Street
London SW1W 0LT
England
In association with
Watkins Bookshop
21 Cecil Court
Charing Cross Road
London WC2N 4HB

ISBN 0 7224 0144 2

Printed in Great Britain

CONTENTS

Letter to a Colleague p vii
I The Aged Voices p3
II Possessions p15
III Patience p25
IV Feed My Sheep p35
V The Daily Bread p45
VI Who Lives Here? p55
VII The Perfection of the Life p63

Biblical references are to
the Revised Version

LETTER TO A COLLEAGUE

Dear M,

You once asked me if I could summarize the philosophy which we had so often discussed in our conversations. We felt, you will remember, that the events of life have a significance beyond the mere performance of the daily round, and sought to reconcile this intuitive belief with the necessary and often exciting discharge of one's conventional responsibilities; but to achieve this it is essential to shift one's psychological centre of gravity.

Suprisingly, one finds clear formulations of this requirement in the Gospels; but by custom, and often indifferent translation, many of the sayings have become stale expressions of abstract morality. A closer examination of the original text discloses unexpected meanings which transcend the sterile interpretations of habit.

By their very simplicity, in fact, these ideas inspire the varied and often troubled experiences of life with a certain quality of delight which I find refreshing, as I hope you will also.

J.H.R.

I : THE AGED VOICES

WE ARE ALL FAMILIAR WITH those sorry individuals whose meaning is derived entirely from nostalgic memories of earlier and supposedly happier days. We say disparagingly that they are 'living in the past', and have little patience with them. We are too fully occupied with the problems and excitements of today to be over-concerned with what has gone before. Yet this hypnotic present is really entirely conditioned by our past.

This is an arresting idea, which we do not accept very readily. We believe that we have freedom of choice in our daily activities, but actually all our behaviour is based on the unconscious application of past experience. Consider quite simply how we are aware of the world in which we live, and the people in it. This is derived entirely from impressions received from moment to moment by the physical senses. Without these we should know nothing. Yet these impressions, in themselves, are meaningless. They simply supply factual information of the situation which can only convey meaning when it is suitably correlated by the brain in accordance with patterns of association acquired by experience.

To take a simple example, there is outside my window what I recocognize as a tree; but all that my eyes see is a conglomeration of form and colour which my brain has been educated to interpret as a tree — and specifically an oak tree in leaf. My ears may be assailed by a transient cacophony of sounds which I interpret from experience as the noise of a passing motorcycle. These, and many other recognition patterns have been acquired very early in my life, and thereafter operate automatically and instantaneously without my volition. At every moment, in fact, there is a vast influx of impressions of varying character. Most of these are ignored, but those which are relevant are translated by my brain into meaningful form, and make me aware of the situation.

However, this is only the beginning of the operation, for where the information is significant, the brain equally automatically directs appropriate action. This may be instinctive, as when the hand is rapidly withdrawn from a hot surface, but the greater part of its activity is concerned with the intricate sequence of feelings and thoughts which is set in motion by the events of life, often accompanied by physical expression or action.

In the ordinary way we assume that this activity is directed by conscious intention. Actually it results from an automatic response of the brain to firmly established programmes laid down in an almost forgotten past. We learn by trial and error how to contend with various situations, and this the brain remembers and applies or adapts to subsequent events. This is not only convenient but necessary in everyday life. Think how awkward it would be if we had to work out our actions in detail every time we wanted to walk across the road, or carry on a conversation. Similarly the many intellectual and emotional judgements which have to be made in the course of the day are all performed automatically in accordance with established programmes.

Were it not so, life would be chaotic. We should be quite unable to cope with the rapidly changing events. Indeed, the better the quality of the programming the more competent our behaviour. As experience develops, the response pattern may be modified to some extent, but our behaviour in general is determined by the unconscious use of a wide variety of programmes established in the recesses of our past.

This astonishingly intricate mechanism, which we take so completely for granted, is really very indifferently used. The customary stereotyped associations permit us to contend reasonably well with the sequence of events, though we make many difficulties for ourselves by the unconscious response to a variety of unnecessary programmes concerned with anxiety, greed, envy, what people think of us, and so forth; but by and large it works, and we are sustained by the illusion of progress.

Yet this is a sterile pattern, for as long as the same programmes are used, the quality of one's experience must remain the same. Even apparently new situations are still interpreted by the aged voices of the past, so that one's experience is characterised by continual repetition.

Really fresh experience can only be achieved by the creation of new response programmes which provide different interpretations of events. This involves a change of outlook which the Gospels call *metanoia* — inadequately translated as repentance, which means re-thinking, but by custom the meaning has become degraded to imply regret for one's misdeeds which is a futile exercise. The real meaning of the word metanoia is expansion of the *mind*, but to understand what this implies we must clarify our idea of the mind.

Our awareness of the world, and our reactions to events, are determined by the brain, which is a remarkably sophisticated computer of wonderful potentiality; but despite its intricacy it is no more than a physical mechanism which can only operate in response to directions which have been laid down initially by an intelligence of a superior order. It can, in fact, only do what it has been instructed to do (though these very instructions may permit a certain independence which creates the illusion of free will).

It is the provision of these basic directions, or programmes, which is the function of the mind, and this is not part of the physical mechanism, but is an attribute of the spiritual body which is the mainspring of man's real structure (as is discussed in Chapter 6). However, for the maintenance of physical existence only a minimal attention is required, so that the mind goes to sleep. This is the real meaning of the many references to sleep in esoteric literature, and if the mind is to exercise its proper potentialities it must be awakened from its complacent slumber.

This requires a conscious recognition of the conditions of our existence, not in a critical spirit but as an objective appraisal, accompanied by an acknowledgment of the superior intelligence which directs the mechanism. With this greater (and more humble) awareness it becomes possible to see that while the customary reactions have a certain necessary but limited usefulness there are other more significant interpretations which can operate *simultaneously* with the established patterns of habit.

There is an indication of this requirement in the well-known parable of the prodigal son, though this is usually interpreted at a wrong level. It depicts a young man who claims his portion of his inheritance and sets out for a far country where he squanders his substance in riotous living, and is reduced to a state of penury. In abject despair he crawls back to his father, where he receives an astonishing, and one would think quite undeserved welcome.

The text is found only in Luke (xv, 11-32) where it is recorded in quite uncharacteristic detail, for the parables in general are very succinct. One has the feeling that it has been unnecessarily embroidered, which masks the real meaning. It is an allegory of a man who takes his inheritance — literally what belongs to him — and endeavours to use it for personal gain. (It is not concerned with worldly possessions, for which a different word is used.)

However, in time there develops 'a mighty famine in that country'. The spurious excitements of success no longer satisfy him, and he finds himself spiritually bankrupt. At which point he is said to have 'come to himself' and begins to recall the more significant meanings of his Father's Court which he had forsaken. He resolves to return, and immediately messengers are sent to greet him and provide the nourishment which has been available all the time, but which he was unable to receive in his state of self-interest.

This is the real significance of the parable, for he has *himself* to turn his face in a different direction and submit to the influences of a superior level. Moreover, it appears that this surrender fulfils some special cosmic requirement, for the elder brother who had remained at home is depicted as being very resentful of the special treatment accorded to the returning prodigal. But his Father says 'Son, thou art always with me . . . . but this thy brother was dead and is alive again'.

Now allegories and exhortations cannot exercise their magic until we have created in ourselves something with which they can combine. So we must try to understand in practical terms what is meant by the Father's Court. It clearly relates to a superior level which we have to recognize as actually existing *together with* the world of the flesh. All ordinary knowledge and reasoning, which may be highly sophisticated at its level, is based on associations which are primarily derived from the evidence of the physical senses. But these are known to have a very limited range of perception and so can only present a restricted view of a Universe of vastly greater magnitude and intelligence.

Once this is accepted, the mind can transcend the limitations of habit and begin to create new associative patterns which provide an enrichment of meaning. These new interpretations do not replace the old ones but operate in addition, for the mind and brain have potentialities far greater than are normally utilized. We become aware 'out of the corner of our eye' of a whole new world which we are normally too preoccupied to afford more than a perfunctory acknowledgement — the world of trees and flowers, of birds and animals, of microscopic organisms, of the stars in their courses — all fulfilling their appointed roles in a living Universe of which we are a not very significant part. Truly, as has been said, 'a man wrapped up in himself makes a damned small parcel'.

There is no need to elaborate this idea, for it is evident that the Universe goes about its business without reference to our puny selves. At first some effort is necessary to divert our attention to these extraneous activities, but gradually we begin to experience this increased awareness *simultaneously* with the necessary performance of our ordinary duties, which changes the whole quality of the day.

II : POSSESSIONS

T HERE IS A SIGNIFICANT anecdote in Matthew (xix, 16) concerning a young man who asks 'Master, what good thing shall I do that I may have eternal life?' Christ says rather brusquely 'Why ask me about good? If you want to enter into the life' — literally, to will the consummation of the life — 'keep the commandments'. He does not say *eternal* life, implying that the first requirement is to participate responsibly in the present life and endeavour to fulfil one's duty to society. The young man says, with a certain humility, 'All this I have done; what do I still lack?' To which Christ replies 'If thou wouldest *be perfect*, go, sell all that thou hast, and give to the poor . . . and come, follow me'; and the young man is said to have gone away sorrowful, for he had great possessions.

This is usually interpreted as an injunction to disavow all worldly goods, and withdraw from life — an interpretation which is reinforced by the following passage stressing how hard it is for the 'rich man' to enter the kingdom of heaven. But this is a misleading juxtaposition of two separate episodes. The young man is told to go into life and learn how to use it, which is a practical exercise, and more acceptable to the higher level called the kingdom of heaven, as indicated in the parable of the prodigal son discussed in the previous chapter.

The clue is to be found in the reference to 'possessions', for which a particular word is used in the original text which signifies *what is already established.* It comes from a root ($ὑπαρχω$) meaning to take for granted, so that the passage refers to the wealth of long-established habitual associations so firmly entrenched and unquestioned in the customary reactions to events.

These the young man is told to sell. Yet selling involves exchange, conventionally in terms of money, for personal gain or convenience. Psychological possessions are not so readily negotiable. It is often expedient to modify some attitude which has been observed to cause trouble in our relationships with others, but this is no more than a change of form; and to try to discard completely the established associations of experience would be neither practical nor responsible.

Some different kind of exchange is required, and in the original text there is an additional word which is lost in the customary translation. This is the word $ὑπαγε$, which means to bring under authority, so that the selling or disposal of these established programmes must be subject to the direction of a higher intelligence. This is a very different interpretation, containing no element of personal gain — a situation quite foreign to our customary complacency, which is always conditioned by expectation of reward.

If we are inspired by esoteric or religious ideas to contemplate the surrender of some of our cherished possessions, we do so only in anticipation of substantial personal benefit. But this very expectation is part of the hypnotism of life, and is actually the first (and easiest) of our possessions to be sacrificed. You cannot bargain with God.

There is reward, but it is of a different quality which only emerges as we begin to sacrifice personal values. This is exemplified in the story of Abraham who was told by God to take his only son, Isaac, into the land of Moriah and there to sacrifice him for a burnt offering on a mountain which would be revealed to him (Genesis xxii). This he obeyed, not questioning why he had been so commanded, and prepared his son on an altar. But at the last moment, even as the knife was raised for the slaughter, he was told to stay his hand and substitute a young ram which had become entangled in a nearby thicket; and Abraham 'called the name of that place Jehovah-jireh which means In the mount of the

Lord it shall be provided'.

This indicates the complete sincerity with which one's possessions must be sacrificed to the superior authority which one recognizes as transcending personal evaluation. To sacrifice is to make holy, which implies an understanding of scale, and an awareness of the proper place of the activities of life. Hence to sell what one has involves the conscious surrender of the undue importance assigned to one's possessions — both physical and psychological.

This aspect of the situation is illustrated in a discussion by Christ with his disciples on the subject of anxiety recorded in Luke (xii, 22), which includes the well-known injunction 'Be not anxious for your life'. He reminds them of the birds of the air and the lilies of the field, which are content to display their glory by the direction of a superior intelligence, with no thought for the morrow. Why this faithless *over-concern* with the events of the day? So again He says 'Seek ye not what ye shall eat and what ye shall drink; neither be of a doubtful mind . . . Your Father knoweth that ye have need of these things'.

The admonition not to be of a doubtful mind is particularly interesting, for the word in the original ($\mu\epsilon\tau\epsilon\omega\rho\sigma\varsigma$) implies *expectancy*, which stultifies the understanding. Play the cards as they fall without judgement. This starves the twin devils of fear and meritoriousness, and permits a response to real influences.

Finally comes the injunction 'Sell what ye have, and give alms' — a more significant phrasing than in Matthew, for the word 'alms' (ἐλεημοσυνη) has the quality of mercy and compassion. It refers not to external charity, but to the poor in oneself — the conscious understanding which is normally so inadequately nourished.

We have little mercy for ourselves. Our most treasured possession is the belief that we are 'honourable men', and any failure to match up to this standard induces a sense of guilt which can be very destructive. Yet as we have seen, our behaviour is entirely conditioned by the established programmes of experience, so that despite our illusions to the contrary, we react in the only way we can.

But events are not an end in themselves. If we can weaken this attitude of expectancy we begin to see that all experience is part of a purposeful pattern in a Universe which is not designed for one's personal comfort. The habitual reactions are seen as a necessary part of this role, to be played without judgement but with a certain measure of understanding.

Anxiety is defined as a solicitous desire. In the Greek a two-part word is used derived from $\mu\nu\alpha o\mu\alpha\iota$ — to be mindful — with the prefix $\mu\epsilon\rho\iota$, implying the playing of a part. To be mindful is right and necessary; but instead of performing this objectively, our reactions are adulterated by a host of imaginary fears and judgements. This prevents the proper playing of the role, and distorts the pattern so that the real value of the experience is lost.

We have ample opportunity to observe these useless anxieties, not just in fearful anticipation of events (which may not happen anyway) but in the continual speculation as to whether we have acted wisely or creditably, which is really of very trivial significance. St Paul expresses this when he says 'Happy is the man who judgeth not himself in what he has undertaken', (Rom xiv, 22). Censure is a denial of understanding.

We need to make something more stable in ourselves, which can combine differently with the impact of events; and until this is formed, the same situations will recur indefinitely. This is called having salt in oneself, from which one might envisage a more conscious playing of the role; but there must be in this no feeling of self-satisfaction, for this destroys its quality. As Christ says 'Have salt in yourselves; but if the salt hath lost its savour, wherewith shall it be

20

be seasoned?' (Mark ix, 50).

There are so many things which we understand in our heart but interpret wrongly by our intellect. Yet by these very failures we can learn. As Samuel Butler said in the well-known, but often misquoted line, 'Tis better to have loved and lost than never to have lost at all'.

III : PATIENCE

THERE ARE MANY APHORISMS concerning patience, which is considered to be one of the cardinal virtues. The dictionary defines it as calm endurance, an interpretation which conventionally involves expectation. We know only too well that our aims are rarely capable of instant achievement, so that we learn to wait with resignation for the fulfilment of our desires. We know too, from experience, that the events of life are on a pendulum, continually swinging from one extreme to the opposite. At times things go well, at others badly, and life is full of these pendulum swings of varying amplitude and duration. We are usually only conscious of the periods of frustration when we await hopefully for improvement. We are not so aware when conditions are favourable, so that the inevitable down-swing takes us by surprise.

We accept these fluctuations as part of the natural order of events. We recognize that, in the words of Ecclesiastes, 'To every thing there is a season and a time to every purpose under the heaven', and exercise a superficial patience in our endeavours. Yet real patience is more than a Micawber-like waiting for something to turn up. It involves an awareness of the underlying pattern which our habitual attitudes do not recognize.

This is because at a very early age we fall under the spell of passing time, so that we do not see the life as a whole but only in the successive appearances of the present moment. Nevertheless, in retrospect one can see that all one's experience conforms to a certain recognizable pattern, and this is the real life which is developing by the passage of time.

A significant corollary of this idea is that we do not exist in isolation. Everyone has his or her own 'long-body', or 'time-body' as it is sometimes called, and our individual experiences are the result of interactions between the time-bodies of the many people with whom we come in contact. These conjunctions are not confined to the present moment, but operate within the timeless realm of Eternity. As an example, we sometimes find a happy relationship with someone which is interrupted by the exigencies of life; yet we may meet them years later and find our understanding unimpaired (provided that it has not been destroyed by vain regrets).

Patience, then, involves an awareness of these unmanifest patterns, and of one's own pattern in particular. Our senses portray events as arbitrary and disconnected, though we learn by experience to recognize certain sequences of cause and effect which we endeavour to utilize intelligently. But there are more subtle influences derived from the pattern of the real life which are not interpreted by conventional reason. Sometimes we catch a glimpse of this unmanifest direction when an event which at the time appeared catastrophic is proved subsequently to have been the best thing that could have happened.

Once the existence of this real pattern is accepted, even though it is initially far from being understood, new relationships and possibilities begin to appear in the kaleidoscope of life. It becomes possible to await the unfolding of events without the customary anxious expectancy, and thereby to savour impressions of the present moment which are ignored in the feverish pursuit of desire.

This is patience, — an impersonal state quite different from resignation, having the quality of stillness.

There is an apt poem which runs:—

> 'Where shall wisdom be found?
> Be still and know.
> Seek the strength of no desire.'

(From *The Flame in the Heart* by C.E. Bignall)

Christ says in one place 'In your patience ye shall win your souls'. (Luke xxi, 19.) But the word translated as souls means literally life or spirit, and is the same as is used in the anecdote of the young man discussed in the previous chapter. Hence the implication is that by the exercise of patience one can make the life one's own. The word for patience is from a root (ὑπομενω) meaning to stand firm or to submit. This at once implies the impersonal recognition of a higher authority, which is quite different from contriving.

The phrase appears in an unexpected context at the conclusion of a prophecy of the forth-coming end of the aeon — not the end of the world, but the completion of the age. 'Nation shall rise against nation, and kingdom against kingdom: and there shall be great earthquakes, and in divers places famines and pestilences; and there shall be terrors and great signs from heaven'. These are conditions increasingly prevalent today which one tends to regard with apprehension; but they must be understood as part of a cosmic plan in which we have to participate; which we can do either as uncon-scious puppets or, more significantly, by awakening the individual response to higher levels of intelligence.

So Christ says 'Settle it therefore in your

hearts, (and) not meditate beforehand how ye shall make answer'. The word in the original translated as meditate means to reckon up or calculate, which is an exercise of the logical mind; and this cannot understand the real pattern.

Patience is akin to faith, which is usually defined as belief in authority; but it is more than belief. It rests on the sure and certain knowledge of the superior, but unmanifest, intelligence which directs all the interplay of the phenomenal world. St. Paul defines it more comprehensively in the Epistle to the Hebrews (xi, 1) where he says 'Now faith is the assurance of things hoped for, the proving of things not seen . . . By faith we understand that the worlds have been framed by the word of God, so that what is seen hath not been made out of the things which do appear'.

This we know in our hearts — i.e. in the deeper, but slumbering levels of the mind which are not enslaved by the hypnotism of the senses. Moreover, the word for faith, $\pi\iota\sigma\tau\iota\varsigma$, comes from a root meaning to obey, so that this innate assurance includes the understanding and willing acceptance of the structure of authority in the Universe.

The myriad manifestations of the phenomenal world throughout the vast range of organic life (and the very atoms of material structure) all conform to this requirement in their respective spheres, *and are content therein.* Man in his preoccupation with his own desires is not so content, and wastes his energy in the activities of self-interest, which the Universe does not require, and can only use as ordure.

If we can begin to respond to the innate awareness of a superior level the experiences of life acquire a new quality. The right and proper pleasure in the competent performance of the normal duties begins to be accompanied by a sense of delight as a participant in a Universe of greater stature, in which everything has its place and purpose.

We assume that we possess both patience and faith. This is clearly not so, for what we take to be patience is no more than expectation, while faith is merely belief. Both are qualities which in our normal state only exist in vestigial form and need to be actively nurtured if they are to develop. This commences with the acknowledgement of the existence of the unmanifest pattern, which we know in our hearts but have forgotten. At first this is necessarily an intellectual exercise, but it leads to the creation of new associations; and as we begin to employ these in the interpretation of events, we receive increasing help from influences of a higher quality.

This produces a different assessment of the daily round. We no longer seek to escape from the situations presented to us, but begin to find in them new and more vivid meanings.

IV : FEED MY SHEEP

THERE IS A CURIOUS EPISODE recorded in the Gospel according to St. John (xxi, 15) in which Christ three times asks Peter 'Do you love me', which Peter affirms with increasing earnestness. The incident is only found in this fourth Gospel which was written much later than the other three — about 100 A.D. — by a John who never met Christ, and is believed to have belonged to a school of Bhakti Yoga. Hence it often conveys a deeper emotional understanding of the teaching, and is less concerned with the historical narrative of the synoptic Gospels.

What then is the significance of this apparently pointless repetition? Actually the three questions are not identical, for in the Greek there are two distinct words for love. Christ's original question uses the verb ἀγαπάω (agapao), which has a special meaning implying compassion. This itself is a word we use rather superficially to denote pity; it really means feeling all together, and so involves a conscious understanding. Peter's reply uses the word φιλῶ (philo) which has the quality of personal affection, the conventional emotion of pleasure and appreciation of a person or thing; and Christ says 'Feed my lambs'.

A second time Christ asks the question, still using the word denoting conscious love, but

Peter's response is again on the personal level, evoking the response 'Tend my sheep'.

The third time Christ accepts Peter's lack of understanding, and uses the word $\phi\iota\lambda\omega$, and when Peter, aggrieved by the insistence, protests his love even more earnestly, Christ says gently 'Feed my sheep'.

Now this episode, which in its context appears to be no more than a casual reminiscence, is actually of great practical significance. In the first place it is concerned with two different qualities of that much-abused word 'love', which Peter at his level does not understand — any more than we do in our ordinary activities. The customary interpretation of the word is entirely subjective, and very indiscriminate. We use the same word to describe our liking for a dish of strawberries as for the affection we feel for our family or children — two very different kinds of experience. Yet all these emotions, even at their most idealistic level, are purely personal.

Conscious love is an objective emotion, not adulterated by personal feelings. It is quite foreign to our ordinary experience, and involves a less egocentric awareness of real relationships, not merely between individuals, but within the structure of the Universe as a whole. It is, in fact, concerned with the understanding of the underlying pattern discussed in the previous chapter.

This is difficult to achieve because, as said earlier, our normal reactions are unconscious. Every situation is assessed by reference to long-established associations which determine what we call our Personality. We believe that we are in control of this behaviour and are responsible for the various decisions and actions. Actually, these are no more than automatic and unconscious responses to programmes which have become adulterated over the years by the inordinate requirements of self-interest, which blind us to the real situation. It is as if the Personality were populated by a motley collection of irresponsible automata, concerned only with their personal ambitions, who come into action 'on cue' without any overall direction; and each of these we invest with the feeling of 'I', despite the fact that they are often inconsistent and even contradictory.

It is, moreover, these little 'I's' which determine our assessment of other people. We do not see them as they are, but only as they impinge on our preconceived notions, which is a very insecure relationship, easily disturbed by anything which upsets our self-esteem. Consider

37

how easily liking can be turned into distaste, or even hatred, by some arbitrary and often trivial event. Small wonder that the world is so full of bitterness and misunderstandings.

The situation is not irremediable, but it can only be changed by the provision of different associative programmes. However, this requires the direction of an awakening mind, not trammelled by the stereotyped attitudes of the past. This leads to the creation of 'I's' of a superior quality which can recognize relationships of a different order. Clearly this cannot be achieved overnight, but can only develop gradually as the result of an increasing surrender to influences of a higher quality.

With this in mind the injunction 'Feed my sheep' acquires an unexpected significance. There are many references to sheep in the Gospels, perhaps because the rural community of the time would be well aware of the wayward character of these animals which are easily led astray and lack any intrinsic leadership. They have, in fact, to be looked after by a shepherd. Hence these references are customarily interpreted as implying the need to provide spiritual guidance for humanity at large.

However, there is an alternative interpretation of more individual significance, in which the sheep are representations of the innumerable I's in our Personality, which are undeniably capricious and lacking any real leadership. Yet they *can* be directed, and it is of significance that in the original Greek there is again a special usage. The usual word for sheep is ὀιος, but in this context the word used is προβατον (probaton), which is defined as 'anything that walks forward' — a root from which our word probationer is derived. Hence there is the implication that these sheep can proceed in an orderly manner if they are suitably directed.

A physical shepherd is clearly of a superior intelligence to the flock he directs, though there are sometimes certain individual sheep who res-respond more readily to his direction and to this extent can lead the remainder. There is a similar relationship in the psychological situation. The direction is provided by an intelligence superior to that which suffices for the normal mundane activities, but this must be exercised by the deeper levels of the mind. This provides new programmes which are implemented by I's of a different quality, and which can thus begin to exercise a certain leadership.

Actually these I's are formed very early in life and create the sense of wonder and delight which we experience so vividly in youth; but these are over-ridden by the supposedly more important requirements of life, so that they become starved. These are the sheep which have to be fed — the lost sheep spoken of in the Gospels, for which the shepherd makes such diligent search. They have not only to be found, but led into new pastures where they can be adequately nourished and so grow in stature.

They are, of course, not at the level of the shepherd, being of an intermediate quality. At first they are inevitably tinged with the expectation of reward, though possibly no longer in terms of life ambition. However, in due course this has to be surrendered to make room for a simple, and quite impersonal delight in the pattern of existence. This is a state of bliss — a word used by the Greeks to describe the condition of the gods, to attain which it is said that a man must 'lose his soul', i.e. his preoccupation with himself and his conventional ideas of value and merit.

This impersonal state is mentioned by the late Maurice Nicoll in one of his Commentaries, in which he says 'As we cease to *invent* ourselves, so we cease to invent other people . . . We begin to *feel* a common existence which is without passion, and is simply what it is, without further definition'. The idea that we invent ourselves and others is a very salutary shock to our customary complacency.

Now while we can comprehend the possibility of different levels of experience, we tend to regard the state of bliss as relevant to some future existence. This is not so, for the pursuit of enlightenment is an entirely practical and immediate exercise. We are not suddenly translated to a higher plane, but by patience we may occasionally be given moments of more vivid experience. These will not last, for the additional energy is quickly dissipated, but by persistence they may become more frequent, so that a certain rhythm begins to develop.

The reality of these experiences has been confirmed by many writers. They have the quality of re-discovery of our birthright which, like Esau, we have surrendered for a mess of pottage. This was beautifully expressed by Thomas Traherne who, in his *Centuries of Meditations*, recalls the vividness of his childhood experience before his impressions had become distorted by reason.

Briefly he says as follows. 'Adam in Paradise had not more sweet and curious apprehensions of the world than when I was a child. All appeared new, and strange at first, inexpressibly rare and delightful and beautiful . . . I seemed as one brought into the Estate of Innocence. All things were pure and glorious: yea, and infinitely mine, and joyful and precious. I knew not that there were any sins or complaints or vices . . . Everything was at rest, free and immortal. I knew nothing of sickness or death, of poverties and contentions. In the absence of which I was entertained like an angel with the works of God in their splendour and glory.

'Is it not strange that an infant should be heir of the whole world, and see those mysteries which the books of the learned never unfold?'

V : THE DAILY BREAD

I N THE MIDST OF OUR MANY preoccupations with life it rarely occurs to us to wonder how it is that we are alive at all. Yet surely this is a great mystery.

We assume, rather perfunctorily, that life in general is sustained by the intake of food in one form or another, and are content to accept this as a natural law. We may sometimes wonder at the astonishing expertise with which the body transforms physical food into the energies which it requires for its various activities, though again we take this for granted. Actually, the physical aspects of these processes can be reproduced (with some difficulty) in the laboratory, but however sophisticated the technique, it does not create life. Some vital factor is missing.

This very fact is a clear indication of the existence of different levels of intelligence in the Universe. The phenomenon of life on earth, not merely in human shape, but throughout the vast elaboration of living matter, is the manifestation in physical form of an underlying pattern of a different order. The intricate activities are sustained by the interchange of various forms of physical energy (including material substances), but these are all subservient to the influence and utilization of an additional *vital* energy, which is of a higher, and non-physical, quality. Without an adequate supply of this energy the organism dies.

The human body uses a variety of energies, which it creates by a fascinating series of transformations. It takes in physical food, which is digested in the stomach into more refined forms which can be absorbed into the bloodstream to reinforce the continual wastage of tissues. The process is reinforced by the intake of air into the lungs, which produce transformations of a more subtle kind and create the energies of a still more refined quality by which the brain is enabled to interpret the myriad impressions of the senses, not only in terms of action but in the exercise of the functions of thought and feeling.

Now without going into detail it is evident that this process involves a series of transformations of *quality*; but any change of state can only be produced by the influence of a superior level of energy. Water, for example, can be changed into steam by the application of heat, which is an energy of a different order. Hence the successive transformations in the assimilation of food are dependent on the presence of appropriate energies already existing within the body. But these cannot create themselves. They must be enlivened by a superior quality of energy emanating from *outside* the organism itself — the pool of vital energy which animates the whole of organic life. This is a magical situation which we should acknowledge much more than we do. Truly man 'shall not live by bread alone, but by every word that proceedeth out of the mouth of God' (Matthew iv, 4).

Life is thus not an accident. It is sustained by energy from higher levels for a cosmic purpose. Moreover man, as a special creation, has access to other forms of spiritual energy beyond those required for the maintenance of physical existence. Yet this he takes as a right, without any acknowledgement of the responsibility it entails. Humanity at large has no individual responsibility. It is merely part of organic life, directed by the group intelligence of the structure for cosmic requirements. But once a man 'comes to himself', as a result of esoteric influences, he has thenceforward a responsibility; and this must be discharged, or the supply of energy will be withdrawn.

The requirement is explicitly expressed in the well known Lord's Prayer, so often intoned in a perfunctory manner as if the mere repetition conferred some merit. Actually it was formulated by Christ to his disciples as a pattern of the way to approach the higher level called Heaven (Matthew vi, 9).

It starts with the essential acknowledgement of a superior intelligence within the superior level called Heaven. Then comes the strange demand 'Give us this day our daily bread', which is usually taken to imply that the Universe owes us a living. The real meaning is very different, for in the original Greek the word translated as 'daily' has a special connotation which has no easy equivalent in English. The word is epiousios (ἐπιουσιος), which means literally 'for the purpose of what is appropriate'. Hence the phrase is a plea for the continuance of the supply, day-by-day, of the spiritual energy necessary for our development. In the scheme of the Universe, this energy is dissipated daily and has to be replenished; but whereas this should serve a useful purpose, it is not normally profitably used. Nevertheless we pray that the supply shall not for that reason be withheld.

There is here no suggestion of right. On the contrary, there is an enormous indebtedness, as is acknowledged in the subsequent prayer that this debt may be cancelled; for which we offer at least a token payment by agreeing to cancel what we imagine we are owed by life. The wording of the phrase is specific. In the original it reads 'cancel what we owe *to the extent that* we cancel what is owed to us', which is of much deeper significance than the conventional complacent interpretation.

This is the basis of a positive and practical philosophy which should accompany us through life. Prayer is not just a form of words to be repeated at stated intervals (though it is helpful to re-affirm one's understanding in the morning before going forth to meet the day). Real prayer is a continuing state, which acknowledges with gratitude the enlivenment of Heaven and seeks to pay for this precious energy by using it properly.

It is the *use* of this energy which is important, for it cannot be preserved. This is clearly shown in the Old Testament account of the *manna* which was miraculously supplied each day for the Israelites during their sojourn in the wilderness (Exodus xvi, 15); and they were commanded to use it the same day, for if they endeavoured to keep it, it 'bred worms and stank'. There is a similar reference in the parable of the talents (Matthew xxv, 14) in which a man about to go abroad for a time entrusted his goods to three servants according to their ability. Two invested their portion wisely and increased its value, but the third merely preserved his intact; and the master on his return was very angry and dismissed him as an unprofitable servant.

In practice, far from making profitable use of this spiritual energy, we are virtually unaware of its presence. Our physical existence is sustained by the daily influx of vital energy, which is not exclusive to humanity but invigorates the whole of organic life; but man, as a special creation, is also supplied with a daily ration of higher-quality energy which is designed to nourish his *mind*. This energy is not properly used, but is squandered in useless personal activities; and the situation is aggravated by the fact that these crude functions can only use low-grade fuel so that the high-quality energy has to manifest itself as violence. We usually think of violence only in physical terms, but the word really implies profanation, i.e. the use of holy material for inferior purposes.

This is why we have so much energy for the stupidities of life, the miasma of greed and envy, of petty judgments and imagined slights. We harbour resentment against people, and even against the Universe, in the continual belief that we are not being properly treated, so that we live in a constant atmosphere of *objecting*. In this self-imposed prison, from which we are too lazy to escape, we have no real individuality, but are merely part of the mass of humanity fulfilling a purely mechanical role in the cosmic plan.

Yet the door of the prison is open. We have merely to sacrifice the comfortable security of our habitual attitudes and make room for infinitely more meaningful interpretations of the events which are presented to us. For which, by the mercy of Heaven, we are supplied every day with the necessary energy. Once this is acknowledged, and properly utilized we may perhaps begin to acquire a real individuality.

VI : WHO LIVES HERE?

THE MOST STULTIFYING OF the many illusions of life is the belief that we are our body. This is inculcated at an early age and quickly dispels the innocence of childhood. We are taught that we are 'persons', with our own individual thoughts and feelings, which are conveniently expressed for us, with their concomitant actions, by the body; and with this we identify ourselves completely.

Yet the word person comes from the Latin *persona* which means a mask; and we have seen that the body is really no more than a mechanism which receives information via the senses and interprets this in accordance with stereotyped programmes acquired by experience. Moreover — though it will offend our pride to recognize the fact — none of these programmes is our own! They are all second-hand, having all been primarily acquired from other people, either verbally or in books, as part of the normal process of education.

Hence to regard the body as oneself — and still more as the whole of oneself — is clearly nonsense. We have an innate belief that the body is some kind of temporary habitation for an immaterial entity called the soul, which is presumed to be immortal, but this is usually interpreted in abstract terms, having significance only in some mythical future state.

Actually the idea of spiritual body is of the greatest practical and immediate significance, for it is here that our real being resides. If we remember that all the appearances of the physical world are interpretations by the senses of an invisible pattern of a higher order, there is no difficulty in understanding that the physical body is merely a mechanism for establishing a satisfactory relationship to the phenomenal world.

It is a very sophisticated and ingenious mechanism which we accept without any semblance of gratitude; but no mechanism, however cleverly contrived, can function without the direction of a superior intelligence. This lays down the programmes to which the mechanism is required to conform, and to which it then responds automatically. The human body functions so efficiently that it appears to possess its own intelligence, but this is really only the exercise of the established programming.

Some of the programmes, concerned with what we call the instinctive functions, are innate and operate so smoothly that we rarely give them a thought. Yet how does the body know how to digest its food and reinforce the tissues by the circulation of the blood? How does it initiate the rhythmic process of breathing essential to its survival? How does it know how

56

to contend with hostile influences which threaten its existence? This is the more remarkable when one remembers that all this has developed from a single fertilized cell which divides into two, and then again into two, and so on until after some 45 such divisions there is an aggregate of over 25 million million cells! Yet these are not all the same. At some stage in the process certain cells develop specialist qualities. Some form bone, others tissue. Some become liver or kidney. Others form lungs which *later* will breathe, or eyes which *later* will see. There is some overall direction. As Sir Charles Sherrington once said 'It is as if an immanent principle inspired each cell with the knowledge for the carrying out of a design'.

An important part of this process is the creation of the brain, which can then begin to be used for a variety of voluntary programmes, based on experience, which provide appropriate inter-pretations of the information received by the senses. These programmes are *not* innate, and are capable of being modified, though in practice they become as automatic and predictable as those which govern the instinctive functions.

The significant point is that all this activity, both instinctive and voluntary, is directed by intelligences which are not contained in the physical body. They emanate primarily from the consciousness of a spiritual body which belongs to a superior level of the Universe. According to esoteric teaching this is required to develop in a particular manner, for which purpose it has to create a physical body in order to utilize the experiences of the phenomenal world, which are thus not an end in themselves but are a kind of food.

However, the soul cannot communicate directly with the physical level so that it has to create an intermediate intelligence which we call the mind. Part of this is concerned with the instinctive functions, and is for the most part unencumbered so that it operates reasonably successfully. The direction of the voluntary behaviour, however, is not so pure. It quickly becomes distorted by personal interpretations, and because these produce a certain self-satisfaction the mind rests content.

Yet this can only extract a stale and repetitious form of nourishment from the experiences of the life, so that the soul is continually prodding the mind to provide more significant interpretations; but this is very difficult because of the weight of the long-established complacency, and this is its real task.

Hence it is relevant to ask 'Who lives here?' Who is really inhabiting this complex and fascinating edifice called the body? Normally it is populated by a motley crew of warring and self-interested puppets which must be stripped of their spurious authority and made to obey the real master. This is illustrated by the anecdote of Christ clearing the money-changers out of the temple. 'My house shall be called a house of prayer, but ye make it a den of robbers' (Matthew xxi, 13); and prayer, as we have seen, is the acknowledgement of a higher level.

In these terms, one can understand that the soul, which belongs to and is inspired by a higher level of consciousness, is not animated by expectation or judgement. It is aware of the situations as they are, both in physical form and as part of the unmanifest pattern which is not enslaved by the limitations of the senses and the tyranny of passing time. Moreover, it recognizes as part of the pattern the continuing use of habitual programmes which have outlived their usefulness, and is thereby able to suggest, in a way which we can understand, programmes of a more significant character.

If one takes advantage of these opportunities there is a gradual change in the quality of one's experience. It is as if, at last, there is someone at home in the house — as there used to be when we were children; someone *not ourselves* who can show us many wonderful things which we have forgotten.

VII : THE PERFECTION OF THE LIFE

THE FIFTEENTH CENTURY mystic Nicolas of Cusa maintained that right living involved what he called 'learned ignorance'. This is really the key to practical understanding. We have of necessity to use our wits in contending with the conditions of life, but we are intuitively aware that this is only a fragmentary interpretation of a reality of which our ordinary attitudes are indeed ignorant.

It is with this reality that we attempt to communicate by the response to different programmes laid down by the deeper parts of the mind; but it is important to recognize that these new programmes are *not of our own contriving*. It is true that we can, by 'taking thought', develop new associations which provide different interpretations of events, but this is no more than a preliminary exercise. The really significant new programmes are created by intelligences of a higher order, and these can only be effective if we are willing to make room for them by surrendering our habitual forms of thinking.

This is true repentance, which means literally re-thinking. I prefer the original word *metanoia*, because it is not an intellectual exercise but is concerned with the awakening of the deeper levels of the mind which can be directed by higher levels of consciousness in the Universe;

and these are of cosmic dispensation. It is said that man is a special creation within the structure of organic life, which he interprets in his arrogance as implying the ultimate mastery of the phenomenal world. Actually, his special quality arises from the fact that he is equipped to respond to the (impersonal) influences of higher levels; but it is part of the plan that this response is entirely voluntary.

The mass of humanity does not fulfil this potentiality and its energies feed inferior levels of the Universe; but any genuine response to higher influences creates a particular kind of energy which is of significant value to higher levels. This was indicated by Christ in the oft-quoted saying 'There shall be joy in heaven over one sinner that repenteth more than over ninety and nine righteous persons that need no repentance' (Luke xv, 7). As so often, the translation is inadequate, and usually grossly misinterpreted. To sin is, literally, to miss the mark and so fail to fulfil one's potentialities, while repentance, as we have seen, is concerned with the awakening of the mind. The phrase 'to need no repentance' has, in the original, the implication of failure to provide what is needful, while a righteous person ($\delta\iota\kappa\alpha\iota o\varsigma$) is literally one who conforms to custom (and is thereby oblivious to the influence of higher levels).

64

In practical terms, the effort of awakening produces a remarkable enrichment of experience. One sees a host of connections and relationships which are entirely unrecognized by the sleeping mind in its preoccupation with personal desires and ambitions. Yet by its very nature the practice of metanoia must not be undertaken with any expectation of reward. The more vivid perceptions are really in the nature of a gift from higher levels by way of recompense for the nourishment which they receive from a conscious response. Hence although by ordinary standards individual efforts may appear insignificant and even selfish in a world population of over 3000 million, any spiritual awakening produces a quite inordinate contribution to the Universal harmony.

In these terms one can begin to understand what is meant by the consummation of the life of which Christ spoke to the young man. This is the real purpose of man's existence, and is clearly not a matter of personal advancement, either materially or spiritually, but involves an increasing awareness of oneself as a part of a Universe of great majesty and design. We can, and should, savour the experiences of life in their context, and yet begin to interpret all events (whether 'easy' or 'difficult' by conventional standards) as part of a pattern of greater significance. This creates a kind of impersonal delight in the fulfilment of one's role.

This is not a state to be immediately attained. On the contrary, it is a process of repeated effort which has to be maintained throughout the life. It is, indeed, unlikely to be achieved in a single lifetime, so that one can envisage that the development can continue through several lives, possibly as some form of recurrence or reincarnation. Yet if this is so, it will be evident that no progress is possible unless a start has been made during the present life; otherwise there can only be endless repetition.

We need not be unduly concerned with this speculation, save as an indication of the mercy of the Universe, which we should acknowledge with gratitude in our hearts. One can then interpret this feeling in practical terms by a more conscious utilization of the situations of the daily round; and by its very quality this continuing effort becomes a joyous exercise.